# USEFUL QUOTES

ALI ZOKAEE

 FriesenPress

One Printers Way
Altona, MB R0G0B0
Canada

www.friesenpress.com

**Copyright © 2020 by Ali Zokaee**
First Edition — 2020

All rights reserved.

No part of this publication may be reproduced in any form, or by any means, electronic or mechanical, including photocopying, recording, or any information browsing, storage, or retrieval system, without permission in writing from FriesenPress.

ISBN
8-1-5255-6748-3 (Hardcover)
8-1-5255-6749-0 (Paperback)
8-1-5255-6750-6 (eBook)

*BODY, MIND & SPIRIT, INSPIRATION & PERSONAL GROWTH*

Distributed to the trade by The Ingram Book Company

To be able to overcome the struggle that you are dealing with, at any stage of your life, you should be able to understand the process that got you there.

These quotes may not solve the problem but will help explain some part of it, either before, during, or after the dilemma.

The book has been divided into two chapters. The first chapter contains the quotes that I have come up with on my own. Even if they've been said before by other people, I haven't heard them (at least in this format) from any other source. And if there are any similarities, hopefully the original sources will forgive my ignorance.

The second chapter contains words of wisdom from other people—some well-known, and some not.

Some of these quotes are in line with my own opinions, and some have been included based on the fact that they have beautifully been said, even though their factual concept may not be completely accepted.

By going through and thinking about most of these sayings, some of the important uncertainties in life can become less uncertain.

# CHAPTER 1

1. Life is the process of finding the solutions to satisfy your emotions.

2. It's not just about the action; it's about the approach and attitude.

3. If you want to do something, you should find yourself in a do or die situation and choose not to die.

4. Close your eyes and ears, just say and do what you are supposed to.

5. Live in such a way that the one you're afraid of, be afraid of you.

6. Three characteristics will ruin your future:
    A. Fearfulness
    B. Laziness.
    C. Ignorance

7. Either small things make you happy or big things can't.

8. You can tolerate anything, as long as you have positive emotional bonds with it.

9. I want people talk to me about the things that I want to talk about.

10. Just do the things that you have enough reasons to do.

11. In life, you should go low enough to learn how to get back up.

12. Live in a way that you don't wish to be in anyone else's place.

13. Live in a way that you have less regrets in the future.

14. The reason someone hurts you is because they can.

15. Anyone who can hurt you, will hurt you.

16. You are done with someone when you tell them how you feel and they don't get it.

17. Don't just tell people they don't understand, prove it to them.

18. Not seeing people is less harmful than seeing them.

19. Every morning, welcome yourself to the war, because that is where you are going each day.

20. Weak-minded people cannot and do not understand the truth. If they could, they would not be weak-minded.

21. You are the only person in the world responsible for your satisfaction.

22. You don't need to tell your main reason all the time. Tell less important reasons if necessary.

23. The main reason is usually the darkest and the scariest one.

24. You won't die if you don't want to.

25. In life, you usually don't do what you want; you do what you can.

26. Before starting down any new path in life, compare it to your most important and current priority. If you don't want to sacrifice that priority, you are not going to succeed in the new one. Start down the new path only when you are ready for that sacrifice.

27. The problem is not when you hide something from someone. The problem is when you hide something important from them.

28. One sign of strength is how hard your heels are planted on the floor.

29. Go and make it big somewhere else, then you may be considered.

30. Tell the main reason to anyone who you care.

31. Always choose manliness over nicety.

32. You either make progress or care about people's feelings. Choose one.

33. Respect, based on your achievements and not just your age, is what you need as you get older.

34. No one can do everything right, but some people can do everything wrong.

35. You are on the right path when ordinary people ask you, "Do you have emotions?"

36. It doesn't matter what other people think about you or say to you. Some of them don't know where are you coming from, some of them don't know where are you now, and some of them don't know where are you going to.

37. Stupidity is one of the most powerful weapons of durability in this world.

38. The people who need explanation for the concept of different levels in any field, are the people who are at lower levels.

39. Four levels of expression:

    A. What you say.

    B. What you do.

    C. Why you do it.

    D. How you do it.

40. Get old enough to stop making important mistakes.

41. Today's comfort zone will kill you in the future. Always avoid your comfort zone, in every field and down every path of your life.

42. People will respect you, if you know something that they don't. They will admire you, if you do something that they don't. And they will idolize you, if you do something that they can't.

43. Your character is the combination of what you do, what you don't do, and where your emotional bonds are.

44. Always tell the truth, but remember that when you tell the truth to a thousand people, only a hundred will listen to you, only ten will believe you, and only one of them will react the way they should.

45. As long as you don't have the right mentality for a specific field, you can try it, but don't expect any success.

46. You can get anything when you deserve it.

47. Sometimes you don't know what you want, but you always know what you don't want, close your eyes and ears and go the opposite direction of what you don't want.

48. Your target audience holds the only opinions that matter.

49. Sometimes the difference is not just the difference. It also clarifies what is right and what is wrong.

50. Vast majority of the steps that you are taking throughout your journey, will be small steps. Very few steps throughout your journey will be big ones.

51. During the period of "Getting Ready," the only thing you should not think of is having fun. The fun part comes after the harvesting.

52. Cut the extras.

53. When ordinary people like something, they will overrate it, and when they don't like something, they will underrate it. Therefore, it doesn't matter what ordinary people think or say.

54. Satisfaction is a four-step process:
    1. Find out what you want.
    2. Find out what you don't want.
    3. Do what you want.
    4. Stop doing what you don't want.

55. Every six to eight years, is one chapter of your life. Stable and reliable people take the most from each chapter into the next.

56. Be ready for bad and undesirable situations, so that if they happen, you are ready. If they do not, you're going to enjoy your routine life even more.

57. One of the benefits of getting old is that you'll have the potential to make fewer mistakes.

58. The depth of your relationship with someone is related to the amount of obvious beliefs you have in common.

59. Most people do the wrong things right.

60. Don't try to be a good person. Instead, try to be right.

61. Sometimes the way to deal with your problem is by facing a bigger problem.

62. When you get to a certain level, you need to do something.

63. Everyone is hiding something. The difference between the people is the level of the importance of what they are hiding.

64. The first five years of getting close to someone should be the last five years of getting close to them, otherwise you'll be in trouble.

65. Better to be a chic rural than an unstylish urban.

66. For achievement, keep your knowledge at a satisfactory level and your practice at the required level.

67. Whenever you get very angry, it's because you feel disconnected from one or more of your main emotional bonds.

68. What people think is less important than what they say. What they say is less important than what they do. What they do is less important than why they do it, and why they do it is less important than how they do it.

69. When talking to someone, talk about the things that both of you are interested in—not just one of you.

70. In any context, deal with the people who are either at your level or maximum one level higher or one level lower. There will be more understanding, less misunderstanding, and less harm.

71. My first goal in life is doing what I like and becoming efficient at it; my second is to die from natural causes.

72. Don't break all the rules; just break the ones that need to be broken.

73. The world is not responsible to understand you; you are responsible to understand the world.

74. Always laugh inside, not outside.

75. Life doesn't joke around with anyone, so you don't joke around with anyone either.

76. To make more progress, if your mind is somewhere else, physically be there as well.

77. The most undesired and unplanned part of your journey may become the trademark of your journey.

78. If you are not getting angry at people who don't comply with the things that you think are important to you, it's because they are not really important to you.

79. Don't worry about your future mistakes. When your mistake bucket gets full, you won't make any more.

80. Whenever the trend or brand becomes more important than the actual work, the quality drops.

81. At any level in any field, people think they are doing the right thing, until they see someone who actually is.

82. Isolate yourself from anything unrelated to your path.

83. Before being able to have a good life, you need enough regrets.

84. You are alone when no one is thinking about you.

85. A good person is not someone who does more good things but is someone who does fewer bad things.

86. I don't mind wearing suits, but anywhere you need to dress up, the quality of the work is low.

87. I want people to know what is important to me and respect me for that. I don't expect them to understand why.

88. The first time you get a fake smile from a girl should be the last time; otherwise you'll be in trouble.

89. What seems to be good in the short term, and turns out not to be good mid-term, will again be good in the long term.

90. Each chapter of life takes six to eight years. You need to focus on any field, task, or subject for at least one chapter of your life to be considered reliable in that field.

91. Keep the necessary distance from anyone you want to keep on dealing with.

92. Any new invention is toxic, but you need a minimum amount of toxicity to be able to live in the society.

93. Everything becomes a job after the first stages of development and excitement, including relationships.

94. When you are young, being cool is important. When you get older, being important is cool.

95. The story of your life will have a different soundtrack than anyone else's.

96. Do everything with feeling, because that's you.

97. Some of your problems will be with you regardless of where you live, because they are specific to your individuality. And some of them will change when you change your situation, because they were specific to those conditions you were involved in.

98. You can live a rebellious life without a rebellious attitude, or a non-rebellious life with a rebellious attitude.

99. You feel guilty when making emotional connections with something outside of your box.

100. People understand the value of you and your work a lot later than what you'd expect.

101. You learn when you are scared enough.

102. You can start several tasks simultaneously, but you can't finish them simultaneously.

103. Unfortunately, it makes sense. But I wish it didn't.

104. Anyone who you listen to, you will end up behaving like them.

105. Don't pay ransom.

106. Your relationships stay healthy for, at best, one chapter (six to eight years) of your life. After that, you still can have that relationship and enjoy it, but a work element or partial separation should be involved, or it won't last.

107. Judge people based on whatever is in their control.

108. The problems are not the people who don't understand. The problems are the people who don't understand that they don't understand.

109. Stick to what makes you feel free.

110. Your character is based on your definition of "The Man."

111. Your biggest problem is usually someone around you.

112. The most painful punishment is telling the truth.

113. I like the people who take the cool works seriously, rather than the people who take the serious works coolly.

114. The world is getting better in the areas that are not important. But it's getting worse in the areas that are critically important.

115. You can do a task correctly, when you judge the people who are either not doing it or doing it wrong.

116. Be only in relationships with people who have something interesting or useful to teach you, or the people who want to learn from you.

117. Don't care about the quantity of your enemies; instead focus on the quality of your friends.

118. What is worse than being too much unorganized, is being too much organized.

119. If you don't have confidence in your field, or are over confident, it's because you have not made enough mistakes in that field yet.

120. Being yourself is more important than getting hurt, so get hurt, but be yourself.

121. Exceptional people in any field are those who've already made all of the possible mistakes in that field.

122. You grow up when you understand that good is not important, and important is not good.

123. It helps if you are clever, work hard, and have talent and luck, but the only important factor for achievement is consistency.

124. Live as an idiot to be able to die as a legend, because if you try to live as a legend, you'll end up dying as an idiot.

125. Don't try to be anything other than yourself—especially funny.

126. My goal in life was finding the fields in which my involvement makes me feel free.

127. Don't speak unfounded words.

128. Not smelling bad is more important than smelling good.

129. If you and your family are healthy, and you have found your path in life, you don't have a major problem.

130. The best moments of life are when you are at a positive emotional balance, which is achievable regardless of many surrounding factors.

131. Regardless of the field, you will hear the truth from anyone who has done something right.

132. I am not weird. Do you know who is weird? The people who are not weird.

133. A test is as good as the percentage of the failure—the higher this percentage, the better the test.

134. When you are a kid, you think that when you grow up you will do everything right. When you are young, you realize that you can't, and when you are a grown up, you know that you shouldn't.

135. My objective is being able to see my distance from the others.

136. A loser is someone who won't progress.

137. One of the most important aspects of life, for a man, is being a man.

138. Being a man is a full-time job.

139. The more simply you deliver a message, the more powerful it will be.

140. The problem comes from the difference in emotional bonds.

141. The second-best moments in life are when you win, and the best moments in life are when you feel free.

142. If you are not loud enough to be worth listening to, no one cares about what you say.

143. Being mature means that, before doing any task, you think about whether you'll have more regret in the future by doing it or by not doing it.

144. Make a mistake when it makes sense to make a mistake.

145. Make only the mistakes that you can afford.

146. Mature as time goes by.

147. Your life starts when you believe the hell on earth.

148. If you need to explain the obvious repeatedly, it's time to leave, because they make you explain many times and they still don't get it.

149. You should be complex enough to attract people, and then stick to simplicity.

150. A movie will move you in the direction that the director of the movie wants you to move.

151. You should focus on your problems based on their priorities, not your abilities.

152. Be the guy that attempts to be as efficient as he can.

153. Ordinary people don't fall in love with the idea; they fall in love with the presenter of the idea.

154. A good boss will tell you what you don't want to hear on a regular basis.

155. Find the sweet spot of each relationship.

156. There are three levels of explanation for a good cultural product:

   A. Giving positive feeling and enjoyment during involvement.

   B. Having an effect and impact.

   C. Making the effect and impact powerful enough that it causes modifications in points of view and behavior.

157. As long as you are young, you need friends, but when you get older, what you need more is respect.

158. Anything that grabs your attention, is because you see the potential in yourself that if you keep on being involved in the same field long enough, you will be ahead of everyone else around you in that field at that point in your life.

159. It's not just about good or bad; it's more about right or wrong.

160. The problem is not just how much you are different from each other now. The problem is how different you will be in the future.

161. I want people to think of me as the guy who understands the importance of simplicity and implements it.

162. Maturity means being able to distinguish between good, right, and important.

163. Everyone is threatened by the danger of being ordinary, until an unbearable incident happens to them.

164. Positive emotional balance is what you want to have every moment of your life.

165. When you are young, your motivation is, getting better. When you get older, your motivation is, not getting worse.

166. It's not just about how much you know; it's more about how much you've absorbed.

167. If it's not simple, it's not powerful enough.

168. As a beginner in a field, you encourage everyone to do what you are doing. As an intermediate, you understand that not everyone can. And as an advanced, you realize that not everyone should.

169. Whatever you do now to satisfy your emotions, carry on a bit, and accumulate to satisfy your future emotions too.

170. Ordinary people are those without enough positive emotional bonds.

171. Truth is harsh. If it's not harsh, it's not the truth.

172. Don't think, say, or do, what you don't mean.

173. Don't listen to anyone who tells the truth. Listen to those who tell the truth and implement it practically in their lives. If they say something that they are not doing, it means they don't believe it deeply enough to take the action. As such, it doesn't matter what they say.

174. The problem is not just that you are not a man yet; the bigger problem is that you are not even on the path to become a man in the future.

175. You grow up when you get hurt, either by your own childish actions or someone else's, to the extent that you emotionally can't tolerate.

176. Good is anyone who has enough positive emotional bonds relative to the situation he is involved in. So, for being good, you should either increase your positive emotional bonds or change your situation, or both.

177. Human beings suck, unless they decide not to and work on it long enough.

178. You are living your life to the fullest potential when the person who you are afraid of is afraid of you, and the person you respect, admire, or worship, respects, admires, or worships you.

179. Your character is based on what you appreciate.

180. Hell is the situation in which you can't have enough positive emotional bonds, and heaven is the situation in which you do have enough positive emotional bonds and don't feel the need to add more.

181. The stronger you are, the less you need to lie.

182. Old fashioned young people are my target audience.

183. Being good is just good and not necessarily important, but being right is important. And good and right are different concepts.

184. When a characteristic in someone is really bothering you, you should do something that people with that characteristic can't do because of that characteristic.

185. It doesn't matter what the other people say, unless they have more knowledge and experience than you in the field that you are involved in.

186. If you keep on doing what the other people are not, eventually you can do what they can't.

187. Forget about finding the easy way; instead, find the right way. And the right way is never easy. If it's easy, it's not the right way.

188. If you hate something, don't kill it. Keep it alive. Its existence increases your value.

189. I don't think everything in the past was good and everything in the future is not. But, I do believe many things in the past were better than many things in the future.

190. Be a noble and free man, with increasingly emotional bonds.

191. How long and how much progress you make depends on the magnitude of your emotional attachment to what you are involved in.

192. Live in a way that you will have fewer regrets later on.

193. There are a lot of meanings in the past, some meanings in the present, and few meanings in the future.

194. Your close friend is someone that you see on a weekly basis, if you live close by, and talk to each other on a monthly basis, if living far apart. Your friend is someone that you see on a monthly basis, if living close by, and talk to each other on a yearly basis, if living far apart. The rest are just acquaintances.

195. Some people are not ready. Some people are not even ready to get ready.

196. What's good for me is not necessarily the right thing.

197. The problem is not just when we are together; the problem is when we are not together.

198. If you are doing better than me, your superior performance is the best critic of my work.

199. You can't go to unrelated places and expect people to respect you at the level that you deserve.

200. There is a hell behind every smile.

201. The thought that being average is good is even worse than being average itself.

202. When you realize the difference between "Need" and "Want", then you can take control of your life.

203. You can't be friends with anyone whose stories are insultingly ordinary for you.

204. Instead of just trying to find your yeses, first try to find your no-no's, then your no's, and then your don't cares. The rest are your yeses.

205. There are many ways to do things wrong, but there are not many ways to do them right.

206. Not only you don't need to be smart to be able to be successful in life, but you also shouldn't be too smart to be able to start the process of being successful in life.

207. The people who are wrong will become more wrong over time.

208. As long as you don't realize something is a problem, you don't have enough reasons to take action to solve it.

209. People don't understand what you think or say, unless you do it long enough.

210. The only thing more toxic than some people is the relationship with those people.

211. When people have the option to do something wrong, they will do it wrong.

212. Always listen to the people who are wrong. By doing the opposite of what they say, you will be on the right path.

213. Either die or get better. And by getting better, this "You" will eventually die.

214. Truth is what you don't expect, you don't want to believe, and you don't understand at first.

215. At any age, make the specific mistakes for that age. At twenty-five, make twenty-five-year-old mistakes. At forty-five make forty-five-year-old mistakes. But if you make a twenty-five-year-old mistake when you are forty-five, then you are a failure.

216. When you stay long enough in a field, you can realize who is telling the truth and to what extent, and who is not telling the truth and to what extent.

217. Some things that are becoming the norm nowadays are the things that should not become the norm.

218. The reason for not being able to make positive emotional bonds with something you used to be able to make positive bonds with in the past, is not just the higher levels of exposure. It is also not enough exposure to the opposite.

219. Each step of the way, you should simulate every aspect of the beginning steps.

220. If you get too uncomfortable when doing something, you are not going to do it long enough. And if you don't do it long enough, you won't get anywhere.

221. You don't realize your weaknesses until you see someone stronger than you.

222. Don't think your serious problems are not big deals. They are big deals, but you should get big enough to deal with them.

223. If something seems easy, it's an indication that you are doing it wrong. Because if you do it right, it won't be easy.

224. Many people can distinguish between good and bad, but most of them can't distinguish between right and wrong until they experience the outcome.

225. The more positive secrets you keep to yourself, and the more negative secrets you reveal, the more emotionally stable you are. The more negative secrets you keep to yourself, and the more positive secrets you reveal, the more emotionally unstable you become.

226. The people who are qualified to criticize, are the people who are busy doing what made them qualified.

227. Meaningful and valuable music and cinema of the past were not just created when social media didn't exist. Back then, they were created because social media didn't exist.

228. You don't need to worry that much if you are on the wrong path. But you should worry if you are on the right path, as that means you are going in the opposite direction.

229. As an observer, you can distinguish between different traits. But as a doer, not that much.

230. When you live long enough and look deep enough, you see similar patterns of degradation, regardless of the field.

231. Usually your problem is not the level of your success but rather the field that you are involved in.

232. You are going to learn more from the people who have failed more.

233. In life, you rarely stand still. You are always moving, which makes it important to choose the right path, otherwise you will be moving in the wrong direction.

234. You are going to have fewer regrets by pretending to be stupid than by pretending to be smart.

235. Lie wins first, not because the truth is not powerful enough but because lie is more attractive.

236. Don't listen to the people who say you should be realistic. Reality is not just what is happening at the moment. It's what happened in the past, what happens now, and what is going to happen in the future, which some people can't see.

237. Find the paths that you are willing to have a geeky approach to.

238. The default mode of human behavior is being weird—unless someone's in a situation that prevents them from being weird.

239. You have less fear when you have less to lose.

240. One of the signs that you are telling the truth is that ordinary people can't tolerate what you say.

241. When you achieve what you wanted to achieve, the process that gets you there changes you to the point that the level of enjoyment you experience is not the same as you had once imagined.

242. What is worse than being always late is being always on time.

243. You don't know how much you appreciate something and how much you detest something until you are done with it.

244. The more truth you reveal, the fewer people you'll attract.

245. Stress from an old source or for an old reason is less bearable than the same level of stress from a different source or for a different reason.

246. One of the few positive elements of the era that we are living in, is that more people distinguish between knowledge and practical knowledge.

247. Truth will not be appreciated if it's not backed by experience.

248. There are positive and negative aspects to every situation and incident. But the ratio of these aspects is not the same, and that's why some are more worthwhile to emotionally invest in.

249. The problem is not doing what you don't want; the problem is doing what you don't want when you need to.

250. Being fundamentally wrong is different than just making some mistakes.

251. As long as your aim is just enjoying your life, this mindset will prevent you from starting the process of doing the right things.

252. Don't look for the people who have made fewer mistakes. Look for the people who have made the same mistakes as you.

253. When you get to a desired point, it doesn't necessarily mean that you appreciate it. What it means is, you used to appreciate it.

254. The further you are from a subject, the stricter answers you are looking for.

255. Life is constantly trying to get everything from you, unless you fight it.

256. Most people don't deserve to be better, and that's why they are not.

257. The people who do better in any field do so, because they do it for real-life reasons.

258. The people who talk more are trying to explain themselves.

259. I am living in a way that mirrors what I wanted a grown-up life to be like, when I was a kid.

260. All of the people regardless of if you are dealing with them or not, including the people who have died in the past, and including the ones who haven't been born yet, have something harsh to tell you in your face, but most of them don't.

261. Social media is the most unnatural and toxic way of human interactions.

262. Most of the things that you enjoy in any field will be enjoyed as long as you keep your distance from them.

263. If you listen to someone with ten years of experience in a field, you'll have the potential to be able to get to ten years of experience in that field. And if you listen to someone with forty years of experience in a field, then you'll have the potential to be able to get to forty years of experience in that field.

264. If someone is not trying to be nice to you, they don't care about you.

265. Being cool is the opposite of being right.

266. You should make as many mistakes as you can when you are young. It prevents you from making those mistakes when you get older.

267. Whenever you choose to go the hard way instead of the easy way, it's because you have a stronger emotional bond to the hard way's destination.

268. You can tell about people's character by what is bothering them and what they consider as problem.

269. People don't understand if they don't need to.

270. There is a difference between weak people and weak-minded people.

271. Weak-minded people do not change their situation even if they have the tools and opportunity.

272. The problem is not just doing something wrong; the main problem is confuse it with the right thing.

273. One of the factors that affects the level of your emotional bond, is how much time you have spent with something.

274. You should have experienced something to be able to present a founded explanation later on.

275. The less you pretend now, the less you are going to be sorry later on.

276. You are going to have less problems with the people who perceive you with the same level of anger that you have inside.

277. If you are concerned about your safety as much as the people around you are, you can't achieve anything in your life.

278. People don't miss the negative signs as often as they miss the positive signs.

279. Being a good person is not a necessity, it's a luxury.

280. Your emotional bond is something that you judge people based on it, otherwise it's not your emotional bond.

281. A problem bothers you as long as you are either searching or implementing the solution process.

282. There wouldn't be any change for positive reasons.

283. Many people are consistent on being wrong.

284. Sometimes your direction is more important than your position.

285. There are a lot more bad music in the world than good music.

286. People's lives have highs and lows. Your highs may not be too high, but your lows will be very low.

287. When you are young, you get identity from any task that you participate in. And as you get older, you gradually will give identity to the tasks that you get involved in.

288. Some people act logically in emotional situations and act emotionally in logical situations.

289. The difference between the people is not just based on the different problems that they encounter, but also the different approach that they take towards those problems.

290. If people criticize you while they are not doing what you are doing better than you, it doesn't matter what they say.

291. The probability that you are not doing what you like because you are afraid, is one hundred percent.

292. Whenever you have to use the word "Just", you are hiding something important.

293. Anyone who you respect in life, have the potential to change your direction.

294. You need to do some work to prevent things from getting worse. And you need to do a lot more to make them improve.

295. Instead of being a funny guy who gets serious sometimes, be a serious guy who gets funny sometimes.

296. You want people appreciate your achievements and not just your personality.

297. When something doesn't work, you don't need to go and find all of the reasons why it didn't work, but you have to go and find out the main reason why it didn't work.

298. The people who say it is not important where you live or what you do, are the people who don't like where they live and don't like what they do.

299. Ordinary person is someone who doesn't have a bigger emotional investment than his relationships.

300. Respectable people and the role models are the people who do the things that they want to get identity from.

301. You can't be a role model if what you do in life is not what you wished you do before starting your adolescent life.

302. Most of the fights and problems are not between the people who have different interests, but are between the people who have the same interest but different approach.

303. Emotional freedom is based on how intense and deep you had made positive emotional bond with something, and how long did it last.

304. Most women don't make a mistake in recognizing the top guy in a field, they make a mistake in recognizing his other areas of competence.

305. Your relationships which break is because either you or the people around you, are inconsistent or are consistent on being wrong.

306. It's not just about taking the best step, it's more about taking the biggest step.

307. The probability that what the inexperienced people say be wrong is so high that worth taking the risk of doing the opposite of what they say.

308. Deal with the people whom your are similar enough that you can negotiate your differences rather than people whom you are too different that you can't address your similarities.

309. You should express yourself partly by your actions and partly by your words.

310. The right way of using social media is, not using it.

311. The level of your success doesn't necessarily depend on the quality of your work, but it more depends on the quality of your advertisement agency's work.

312. One of the signs that you are doing your job properly is not when you attract more people, but when you attract the right people.

313. The reason for improving your baseline is getting more efficient at lower levels.

314. Your ultimate goal in life should be trying not to be average in the fields that you are involved in.

315. The main theme of the past was looking to the future and the main theme of the future is looking at the past.

316. You have a minimum and maximum threshold of tolerance for anything that you encounter in life, find them for the fields that are critically important to you.

317. If you want to achieve anything in life there are two things that you shouldn't think of, safety and balance.

318. You should be different enough to attract the attention and similar enough to be able to hold on to it.

319. Some of the most important things that define your character, are the things that bother you and interest you.

320. When you are young you are supposed to be wrong and as you get older you become less wrong because you get punished by the consequences of your wrong actions.

321. The threshold of success is when people come to you instead of you going to the people.

322. Your appearance tells a lot more about you than any other thought that you pretend to associate with.

323. Which field you choose to follow and what kind of approach you take in that field will reveal your personality, and as you go forward through that field, your personality strengthens.

324. Don't trust the people who smile a lot. They are trying to hide the truth behind their smile. Because truth will take the smile away from your face.

325. The right thing is anything that makes you progress in the positive way.

326. My objective is enjoying my life as much as I can in the confinement of the truth as much as I know.

327. If you divide people into three categories, first the people who listen to same kind of music that you listen to, are easiest to communicate with because you share the same personality, and the closer the music that you listen to, the less you need to explain yourself. Second category are the people who are not musically oriented. Those are the people who are hard to communicate and you need a lot of explanation to be able to deal with them. The third category, are the people who listen to the music that are not meaningful for you. These people are impossible to communicate with, because of the opposition of personalities which manifest itself in the choices of music that they make.

328. A taste in music is a shallow term. The type of the music that you gravitate towards is the manifestation of different aspects of your personality.

329. Most people have both fear of failure and fear of success in different fields. The fields that you have fear of success are the fields that you shouldn't get involved in. Your emotional bond to the outcome of that field is not big enough to move you forward. You should follow the paths that you have fear of failure and not fear of success.

330. If you are ashamed of or can't justify your behaviour to an innocent child, what you are doing is wrong.

331. The bad incidents in your life have more effect on your future than good incidents.

332. The ratio of how much people perceive you based on your achievements and how much they perceive you for your character, differs from time to time and it depends on how much identity you want to get from each one.

333. One of the signs of the average mindset is using extreme adjectives where they are not necessary.

334. "Do you like an art form?" is not the right question. The right question is : "Do you get it or not?"

335. Every field has a continuum, and wherever you are located in that continuum, you consider the people behind you as underachievers and anyone who's ahead of you, as overachievers.

336. Your thoughts, beliefs, and words should have practical implementation in real life, otherwise you are going to bury them with you when you die.

337. Knowing something and experiencing it, are not the same thing. Your credibility is not just based on what you know as much as it is based on what you have experienced.

338. When you know something, you are ahead of the people who don't know it and behind the people who have experienced it.

339. You should listen to people who are more experienced than you in a specific field, but not forever.

340. The difference between knowledge and practical knowledge is, knowledge has the potential to prevent you from falling into the trap, but practical knowledge will prevent you from falling to the trap.

341. With rationality you can't prevent the disaster to happen or even solve the problem after it happened. With rationality you just can explain it to yourself.

342. You should get strong enough to be able to stand in front of bullshit. You can't stand in front of every bullshit but you should do it as much as you can.

343. The reason that you shouldn't wish to be in anyone else's place is because, their current position is the compensation of a big negative emotional bond that they had in the past which you haven't had yet.

344. The main difference between rational people and irrational people is, rational people can explain the process of satisfying their emotions and, act based on deeper emotional bonds, but irrational people act based on superficial emotional bonds and can't explain the process.

345. If you look at anyone who worth looking at, as a role model, they have three or four major emotional bonds that they are involved in at anytime in their life.

346. Average people are a lot weaker than being able to do the things that they know are right, and that's what keeps them average.

347. The purpose of life is becoming a role model in a field and make progress in that field.

348. The less effort you make on getting anything in life the less valuable it will seem in your eyes.

349. In any field as long as you are making small and steady progress, you are on the right path.

350. Having a sense of humour is an important trait, but is not the most important trait that you should have in life.

351. The right way of using the wrong thing is, not using it.

352. If you are average smart, you are not necessarily funny, but if you are above average smart then you will be funny without even you noticing it.

353. Being wise is more important than being funny, and being funny is more important than being clever.

354. The more you are active on social media, the more your life is away from what you want it to be.

355. Having different opinions is not necessarily a deal breaker, what is a deal breaker is having opposing opinions.

356. When you are looking up to someone, you are looking at the destination of the journey that you have already started.

357. Everything you do, say or think is based on one of your emotional bonds.

358. The people who are considered logical, is because their actions and their words are based on deeper emotional bonds relative to the observer.

359. The deeper you dig the more rational you will seem.

360. Every step that you take in life is because the previous step that you took, wasn't big enough to move you far enough from the pain that you are trying to avoid.

361. The ultimate objective in life is not being happy, or smart, or popular, or educated, or wealthy, but it is to get practical wisdom.

362. You are living in a society and you will and should compare yourself to the other people, and even if hypothetically you don't, the whole society and the other people will do it to you.

363. Right is anything that you are not ashamed of doing in front of the eyes or explain it to an innocent child.

364. Everything that happens to you in life is moving you closer to the practical wisdom that you need to have.

365. One of the signs of having the practical wisdom is that you are funny, and if you are not, you haven't got the practical wisdom yet.

366. The people who seem they don't have human emotions, is because they have developed enough emotional bonds either negative or positive when you see them, that to you it doesn't seem any hole left to be filled.

367. The main problem when you are young is not you don't know what is right and what is wrong, but is even though you know the right thing, you don't have enough reasons to do it because you still can afford to be wrong.

368. The reason that you get attracted to someone is the same reason which, that person will make your life a hell.

369. If what you want to do, doesn't have a stronger emotional component than any other activity that you are currently involved in, either don't waste your time or if you do, know that you are wasting your time.

370. For achievement you should fail so many times that you become numb to failure.

371. The less you have something to lean on, the smoother you progress.

372. Right is any attempt with desired outcome and wrong is any attempt with undesired outcome.

373. Practically you will make the least amount of effort that keeps you ahead of the people that you want to be ahead of with your desired margin.

374. The number of the people who get the person that they want at any given time and live happily ever after, is zero.

375. In the beginning you can't do what you want to do, not because you don't have enough motivation but because you don't have the required tools.

376. Your approach throughout your life should be the same, even though the outcome of the same approach will be different in different times.

377. How do you know the limit of your potential? By trying to exceed it and fail. Otherwise you will never know your potential.

378. Every step that you take in life is because the magnitude of your positive emotional bond with the outcome of that step in the future is big enough that makes you take that step.

379. The people who tell you, you can't handle criticism, don't understand that the problem is the criticism that comes from the wrong source, if it comes from the right source, it will be appreciated.

380. The amount of time that you spend on thinking about your past, your present, and your future depends on the level of emotional attachment that you have to each era in your life. The more you think of your past the more afraid you are about your future. The more you think of your future the more painful your past have been. And the more you think of your present the harder your situation is in present.

381. The level of the anger inside you is one of the most important indicators of your identity.

382. You are more comfortable with people who perceive you with the right priority of your identity aspects. And you will have more problem with people who perceive you with the wrong priority of your identity aspects.

383. Any task that you are doing at a specific moment in your life is the most important thing at that moment in your life otherwise you wouldn't be doing it.

384. Most people are very good at making your life a hell.

385. Charm means having made emotional bonds with a source that the others don't have access to, yet.

386. The only reason that someone comes to you is because they haven't seen anyone better than you for the reason that they have chosen you.

387. The farther out you look into the future, the more your behaviour is free will like, and the closer it is to the present, your behaviour is more determined.

388. Half of your achievements depend on your luck and the other half on your efforts.

389. My goal is being able to find the spot that I enjoy my life up to a point that the extent that it prevents me from doing the right things, be minimized.

390. One of the hardest tasks in the world is confronting the people who have caused you trouble, but without this confrontation, your life will be even harder and more unpleasant, so you need to do this confrontation.

391. Your efforts in your field should be impressive enough to motivate intense people to imitate you.

392. If you turn your head away from the main problem and focus on less important problems, you'll commit a crime.

393. All of your problems in the world are the consequences of either you or someone else's weakness at a point in time.

394. Do you know why it doesn't matter what the other people say to you? Because the possibility that they were thinking about telling you something and as soon as they see you, they tell you something else is very high.

395. All of the fights with the girls come back to the question that why you don't have a higher status in your field.

396. The most important part of your identity in the eyes of the other people is your biggest emotional bond that they can see in you.

397. The magnitude of your emotional bond to the destination of the path that you are on, should be big enough to prevent you from thinking of anything else, otherwise that's not your path.

398. The level of your satisfaction depends on the number of no's that you say in life. The more no's you say the more satisfied you will be, and the more yeses you say, the less satisfied you will feel.

399. The older and more qualified you get, the less you need to look for role model and the younger and less qualified you are, the more you need to look for role model.

400. An artist is not necessarily someone who is involved in an art field, but is someone who starts a cultural movement to the extent that people see him as a role model.

401. If you are pure and simple, in the beginning the young people won't like you and the older people don't mind you, but as time goes by, the younger people won't mind you and the older people will like and rely on you.

402. The reason that you are involved in what you are involved in, is because you can't do any better.

403. Being smart is not a necessarily positive characteristic in life, but being wise is.

404. The proper way of living is being on a path that over time the inherited parts of your identity become less and less important.

405. The less similarities and more differences you have in common in important aspects of your identity with someone, the shorter, less joyful and more problematic your relationship will be with that person.

406. The mask that you put on to communicate with the other people is proportionate to the level of differences that you have with that person. The more differences you have with someone the thicker, heavier and bigger mask you need, and the less differences you have, the lighter, softer and smaller mask you can use.

407. You grow up when you see the flaws of the people that you used to rely on to the extent that you can't rely on them anymore.

408. You don't need to make any effort to get exposed to the middle of any curve. But you need to make an effort to get exposed to anything good or anything bad in a field. And the exposure to the bad is as important as exposure to the good because it provides you with the comparison base and increases the value of good in your eyes.

409. The quality of the products of any organization will reveal enough about the organization that can justify its existence.

410. Your starting point and your destination are not in your control, but your path is.

411. Life is a collection of tests. You are being tested on a regular basis, and the result is based on the attitude that you take towards the paths that you choose in life. The people who get the lower scores don't have the right to criticize people with higher scores.

412. If you are not interested in a field, it's because you haven't been punished hard enough by the choices you've made based on the lack of knowledge in that field.

413. Being wrong is right when you are young. But as you get older not only you should be able to distinguish between right and wrong but also you should be able to implement it practically in your real life.

414. Average people are average because they say something and they do the opposite of what they said.

415. Your past is an unsolvable problem.

416. The less you prepare for an event, the less expectations and less stress you will have and you will enjoy the event more and it's going to be more efficient and productive.

417. When doing something for the first time, almost everyone will do it wrong because they haven't been punished hard enough by the consequences of their wrong action yet.

418. The level of your association to each aspect of your identity, should be relative to the level of its importance.

419. The biggest problem regarding human interactions, is the order of different aspects of your identity in your head, compared to the order of those aspects in the other people's eyes.

420. If someone is not motivated, it's because they haven't been punished hard enough by the consequences of their previous actions, because after that they have no option other than being motivated.

421. The level of attractiveness of someone correlates to the level of their honesty. The less someone lies the more attractive they are.

422. You don't get close to someone just because of your similarities, but because of your differences too.

423. Your role model is the destination of the journey that you will start after encountering them.

424. Competence brings confidence and confidence is the key for next level achievement.

425. Just listen to musics and watch movies that are better than silence.

426. The lower the level of stress, the higher the level of your tolerance, and the higher the level of stress, the lower the level of your tolerance will be.

427. Your character is based on what you appreciate. And what you appreciate has been appreciated by some other people before you that are older than you. Those people will become your role models in that field, Because they add more wisdom to what you are pursuing.

428. Doing your best and doing whatever it takes are two different things.

429. The more similar emotional bonds we have made up to this point in our lives, the more similar decisions we will make from this point on in our lives.

430. You make an emotional bond either with the process of what you are involved in, or the outcome of the process, or both.

431. The more you get identity from something, the less you can tolerate people who don't get identity from it.

432. As long as you struggle emotionally, you will struggle in many other aspects of your life. But it doesn't mean that if you don't struggle emotionally, you are not going to struggle in the other aspects of your life.

433. If you move in the opposite direction of dying, you will be on the path to be more alive.

434. When you die you don't move because you can't move. So, as long as you move and improve your moving skills, you are moving away from dying.

435. Life is about moving, either in the right direction or wrong direction.

436. You can always count on the other people's fears and ignorance.

437. As long as you are less afraid than the other people, do more than the other people, or know more than the other people, you are ahead of them.

438. The reason that a girl finds you attractive is based on your status and the reason that she stays with you is how you get to that status.

439. Live in a way that when the other people look at you, they say that's how it should be done.

440. The happier your life outside of a field, the less successful you will be inside the field.

441. The younger you are, the more you should be yourself and the older you get the more you should do the right things.

442. As soon as you find the fields that make you emotionally satisfied in life, you should choose the fields that you are going to sacrifice and forget about.

443. Anyone who you respect, if you get close to them enough, they are going to make your life a hell.

444. What do you want your legacy be? Do that everyday.

445. As long as your approach doesn't change, the outcome won't change either.

446. If you don't get annoyed with average people, you are average too.

447. The closer you are to the stereotype in any field, the more likely you will be successful in that field and the further you are from a stereotype in any field, the less likely you will be successful in that field.

448. Everyone is looking up to someone who is braver than them, knows more than them or are more capable than them. If you don't know more than the other people or you are not more capable than them, be braver than them. Because everyone knows the cause of their misery is the fears that they had in the past which they didn't address.

449. You will hold on to anything as hard as you've achieved it, the harder you achieve something the harder you hold on to it.

450. The more people are afraid of you in the field that you are involved in, the more right things you are doing in your field.

451. Do something that make hair stands on people's skin.

452. The people who say they are happy with their situation are either too afraid to take the action or don't know how to do it, or both.

453. Your most important job when you are young is, making friends and a community, and proving yourself to be worthy enough not only to be a part of the community, but also sometimes as a leader of that community. When you get older your main job is getting respect by specializing in a field, making another community and keep on growing the new community.

454. The community that you belong to and the city that you live in, should be big enough that keeps you motivated to progress and small enough to provide you with enough calmness to be able to progress.

455. When you prove your competence the probability that some people don't get it, is one hundred percent.

456. There is a big difference between your problems and your faults. There are a lot of things that are your problems but are not your faults.

457. Being real sad is more important than fake happiness.

458. If you want to achieve anything first you need to have the right mentality for that field and second you should be around the right crowd.

459. You should listen to people who are wrong and anyone with high level of difference with you, not because you appreciate what they say, but because you see how much wrong and different people than you can survive.

460. Problems can be complicated or simple depending on how deep you look at them. The deeper you look, the simpler they become.

461. If you look at anyone who worth looking at as a role model, they are usually competent in two to four different fields at a time.

462. Being cool is different than looking cool.

463. The more important one aspect of your identity results in an outcome, the better feelings you will have.

464. In any field as long as you don't know more than the people whom you are listening to, you should rely on what they say.

465. In the beginning of your journey you should know and see what is considered to be good to show you your destination and path. But as you progress you should be constantly reminded what is bad, to redirect you on the right path.

466. Your behavioural pattern in one field in your life will manifest itself in some other fields in your life too, if not all.

467. The older you get the more facts you discover in life and as long as you don't try to bypass those facts you will be fine, but every time you try to fight them you will lose.

468. The difference between a desired job and an undesired job is not the unpleasant parts of the job, but is between the pleasant parts of them.

469. Doing the right things doesn't necessarily level you up in the society.

470. The bigger the difference between your level and someone else's, the safer for you to show your weaknesses.

471. The people who ask the wrong questions not only don't know anything about the subject that they are asking, they don't even know what they want to get from your answer.

472. A good music track takes you to an emotional place better than your current place. And a bad music track takes you to an emotional place worse than your current place.

473. The closer your level to someone in a field the more you can relate to them and the further your level from someone in a field the more you can rely on them.

474. As time goes by, there are a lot less role models compared to the past.

475. Some of the best moments of your life are when you get a compliment from someone that you care, either the more advanced people in that field or anyone that matters what they say.

476. Your interests are good and right to follow as long as they don't become your only emotional bond to the extent that you use them as weapons.

477. I prefer to hear less truth from someone whose actions are closer to what they say than hearing more truth from someone whose actions are further away from what they say.

478. You should give the people who hate you because of the truth that you are revealing, as much reasons as you can to keep on hating you.

479. The people who are not controversial, are not brave enough to reveal enough truth to make them controversial.

480. Your objective in life shouldn't be avoiding fights as much as you can, because as soon as you start the process of doing the right things, you will be in fights with a lot of people. Just get better at fighting.

481. The number of the people who can address their first five most important problems in life before they die is very low. So, if you address the less important problems instead of more important ones, it's just because you are too afraid to face the more important problems.

482. Nothing in this world is a joke if you want to do it properly, even telling a joke.

483. What people say doesn't necessarily mean what you think they mean.

484. When something gets big, your main job will be keeping it big.

485. Your focus in life shouldn't just be on the image that you are moving towards, but you should also have enough exposure to the image that you are moving away from.

486. When you expose yourself to something consistently, over time you get desensitized to that thing and your standard level will get closer to the level of that thing, and also you see the negative sides of that thing which you couldn't see before the exposure, and this combination will increase your potential to appreciate the opposite of that thing.

487. The two most important factors that you need to know and implement in any field are first knowing the basics and important aspects of the field, and second the order of their level of importance.

488. Life is usually moving in the opposite direction of what you want it to go.

489. Don't waste your time on movies that you don't feel less stupid after watching them.

490. Don't be afraid of telling the truth, because vast majority of the people who hear the truth, can't implement it practically in their life and they will continue relying on you.

491. The more you prepare for an event the weaker your position will be when you get there.

492. The more you explain something to the people who don't get it, the more resistant they will be and will cooperate less.

493. Avoid the people who get their identity from the aspects that they haven't contributed to.

494. People don't say what they believe in, they do what they believe in.

495. The positive side of becoming a part of the history is people are going to talk about you forever, and the negative side is, as soon as you become the history, your past is brighter than your future.

496. You can evaluate the validity of a test by its percentage of failure, the higher this percentage the better the test.

497. Listen to the people that not only tell the truth but also can back it up.

498. People will rely on you proportionate to the level of emotional bond that you have made in your field.

499. One of the benefits of western culture is not only the strong get the chance to express themselves, but also the weak have the chance to survive.

500. The more obvious parts of your identity should be based on your achievements and not the things that have been handed to you.

501. The farther the people travel to come to see you, the more you have made it.

502. You should elevate your status in the fields that you are involved in as time goes by.

503. Judging the other people is the only reason that makes you get out of your bed when you wake up in the morning and start doing the things that most of them are not enjoyable for you.

504. The reasons that you get involved in the fields that you are involved in, will have some common similarities to the reasons that people whom you get inspired by, got involved in the same fields.

505. Being clever is not very important because I haven't seen many important people who were clever or many clever people who were important.

506. People come to you because of the strengths that you have and will leave you because of the strengths that you don't.

507. Most people are wrong most of the time and that's why you shouldn't take most of the people seriously.

508. Q : What does better mean? A : If you compare any cultural product in the past with its counterpart in the present, this difference can be expressed by the word "Better".

509. How far you go either in the opposite direction of your evolutionary biology and evolutionary psychology or in the same direction, will determine how famous you will be.

510. The more you tell the truth, the better you live, period.

511. The more you live, the more you can relate to the things that once you couldn't, and the less you relate to some other things that once you could.

512. The people who don't want to be judged in a field are at lower levels compared to what they want to be, otherwise they wanted to be judged.

513. Based on the important parts of your identity in your head, you belong to several communities. Your objective in life should be moving towards the top of those communities.

514. Not all parts of your identity have the same weight in shaping your character. Some of them are more important and heavier, and some of them are less important and lighter.

515. The level of the positive emotional bonds that you make with anything that you have control over, should exceed the level of the negative emotional bonds that you get from the things that you don't have control over, otherwise you can't enjoy your life.

516. Tell the truth as much as you know, and the more you live on this planet, the more truth you will discover.

517. It's not like misunderstandings sometimes happen. Misunderstandings always happen. Life is nothing but misunderstandings.

518. Most of the human activities end up being an experiment rather than an accomplishment.

519. People gravitate towards what is relevant to them instead of gravitating towards the right thing.

520. What you need in life is not necessarily your problems being solved, but the hope that they can be solved is what you need.

521. For most of the human endeavours there is no decision making process involved, because they are mostly emotional based transitions.

522. Open minded men are too weak to be closed minded.

523. You have made it in a field as soon as you start to think of the new field.

524. The possibility that you get something easily is low, but the possibility that you can hold on to what you got easily is zero.

# CHAPTER 2

1. Four factors of success :
   A. Decision
   B. Commitment
   C. Commitment
   D. Commitment – Unknown

2. Action speaks louder than words. – Unknown

3. Chop your own wood; it will warm you twice. – Henry Ford

4. The numbers don't lie. – Carroll D. Wright

5. You won't regret if you double check. – Traditional Proverb

6. It's not the size of the dog in the fight; it's the size of the fight in the dog. – Mark Twain

7. Beggars can't be choosers. – Traditional Proverb

8. Where there is a will, there is a way.
   – Traditional Quote

9. A wayfarer is not going fast and then stops; he goes slow and steady. – Traditional Proverb

10. Anyone who won't eat your bread won't call your name. – Traditional Proverb

11. The innocent's head will get to the gallows but won't be hanged. – Traditional Proverb

12. Thoughts become words, words become actions, and actions become habits. – Lao Tzu

13. Do the thing you fear the most. – Mark Twain

14. Don't fear the loud one, but fear the quiet one.
    – Traditional Proverb

15. Your coworker can be your friend, but your friend can't be your coworker. – Hassan Zokaee

16. The greatest trick that Satan has played is to convince us that it doesn't exist. – John Wilkinson

17. You can fool some people sometimes, but you can't fool everyone all the time. – Jacques Abbadie

18. Don't postpone today's work for tomorrow.
    – Traditional Proverb

19. Healthy skepticism is the basis of all accurate observations. – Arthur Conan Doyle

20. If you don't like my bad behavior, don't give up your good one. – Traditional Proverb

21. If you achieve a higher level, you've already achieved the lower level too. – Traditional Proverb

22. Genius is one percent inspiration, ninety nine percent perspiration. – Thomas Edison

23. A wise enemy is better than an ignorant friend.
    – Traditional Proverb

24. A guest is in the host's hands. – Traditional Proverb

25. The best instructors are the best students.
    – Traditional Quote

26. Mind over matter; if you don't mind, it doesn't matter. – Mark Twain

27. Happiness is the activity, not a state of being.
    – Aristotle

28. Death is not the worst thing that can happen to men.
    – Plato

29. If you bring a thousand reasons for a mistake, you've made a thousand and one mistakes.
    – Traditional Proverb

30. If you don't take the advice from wise people, life will teach them to you in a harsh way. – Traditional Poem

31. You haven't been hungry enough to forget about love.
    – Traditional Proverb

32. Even the darkest night will end and the sun will rise.
    – Victor Hugo

33. There is nothing so powerful as truth.
    – Daniel Webster

34. Everything that exists or happens in the world once was a mental image in someone's mind. – Unknown

35. You should give the devil his due.
    – William Shakespeare

36. The opportunity of defeating the enemy is provided by the enemy himself. – Sun Tzu

37. Unearned wealth kills the feel of the necessity.
    – Traditional Quote

38. Judge a man by his questions rather than his answers.
    – Voltaire

39. Never interrupt your enemy when he is making a mistake. – Napoleon Bonaparte

40. The worst form of inequality is trying to make unequal things equal. – Aristotle

41. If you want something you've never had, you must be willing to do something you've never done.
    – Thomas Jefferson

42. Whenever you find yourself on the side of the majority, it is time to pause and reflect. – Mark Twain

43. Wrong is wrong even if everyone is doing it. Right is right, even if no one is doing it. – Saint Augustine

44. The majority is always wrong, the minority is rarely right. – Henrik Ibsen

45. Many of life's failures are people who did not realize how close they were to success when they gave up.
    – Thomas Edison

46. Without music, life would be a mistake.
    – Friedrich Nietzsche

47. Wrong does not cease to be wrong because the majority share in it. – Leo Tolstoy

48. If you are afraid of being lonely, don't try to be right. – Jules Renard

49. The heights that great men reached and kept, were not achieved by sudden flight, but they while their companions slept, were toiling upward in the night. – H.W. Longfellow

50. Twenty years from now, you will be more disappointed by the things that you didn't do than by the ones you did do. – Mark Twain

51. Every man is guilty of all the good he didn't do. – Voltaire

52. Our worries always come from our weaknesses. – Joseph Joubert

53. Having a hard but real life is better than an easy but a fake life. – Traditional Proverb

54. The authority of a thousand is not worth the humble reasoning of a single individual. – Galileo Galilei

55. Never explain. Your friends do not need it and your enemies will not believe you anyway. – Elbert Hubbard

56. You were born an original. Don't die a copy. – John Mason

57. He has no enemies, but is intensely disliked by his friends. – Oscar Wilde

58. One mustn't criticize other people on grounds where he can't stand perpendicular himself. – Mark Twain

59. The greater the obstacle, the more glory in overcoming it. – Moliere

60. Better make a weak man your enemy than your friend. – Josh Billings

61. Those who know that they are profound strive for clarity. Those who would like to seem profound to the crowd strive for obscurity. – Friedrich Nietzsche

62. This world is a comedy to those who think, and a tragedy to those who feel. – Horace Walpole

63. Life can only be understood backwards; but it must be lived forwards. – Soren Kierkegaard

...

# EXTENDED CITATIONS BY QUOTE NUMBER

2. "Actions Speak Louder than Words." The Free Dictionary. Farlex. https://idioms.thefreedictionary.com/actions speak louder than words.

3. May 21, 1916 St. Louis Post-Dispatch from St. Louis, Missouri • Page 74

4. "Carroll D. Wright". 1852 July 28, The Congressional Globe, 32nd Congress First Session, Page 1956, Column 1, Printed at the Globe Office, Washington. (Google Books full view)

6. Mark Twain Quotes. BrainyQuote.com, BrainyMedia Inc, 2019. https://www.brainyquote.com/quotes/mark_twain_103756.

7. "Beggars Can't Be Choosers." The Free Dictionary. Farlex. https://idioms.thefreedictionary.com/beggars can't be choosers.

8. "Where There's a Will, There's a Way." The Free Dictionary. Farlex. https://idioms.thefreedictionary.com/where there's a will, there's a way.

12. https://quoteinvestigator.com/2013/01/10/watch-your-thoughts

13. "Mark Twain Quotes." BrainyQuote. Xplore. https://www.brainyquote.com/quotes/mark_twain_141714.

16. Wilkinson, J. Quakerism Examined. London, 1836.

17. Abbadie, Jacques. Traité De La Vérité De La Religion Chrétienne. A Rotterdam: Chez Reinier Leers ..., 1684.

19. Vital Message. Project Gutenberg Literary Archive Foundation, 1919.

22. Google Image Result for https://inspirecast.ca/wp-content/uploads/2016/01/Thomas-Edison-Genius-is-one-percent-inspiration-and-ninety-nine-percent-perspiration.jpg. https://images.app.goo.gl/uopvH1N4KzW11Kw2A. quoteresearch, Author. "Genius Is One Percent Inspiration, Ninety-Nine Percent Perspiration." Quote Investigator, October 5, 2018. https://quoteinvestigator.com/2012/12/14/genius-ratio.

26. "Mark Twain Quotes." BrainyQuote. Xplore. https://www.brainyquote.com/quotes/mark_twain_103892.

27. "Aristotle" SparkNotes Editors. "SparkNote on Nicomachean Ethics." SparkNotes LLC. 2003. http://www.sparknotes.com/philosophy/ethics/

28. Plato Quotes. BrainyQuote.com, BrainyMedia Inc, 2019. https://www.brainyquote.com/quotes/plato_395547

32. "A Quote from Les Misérables." Goodreads. Goodreads. https://www.goodreads.com/quotes/10095-even-the-darkest-night-will-end-and-the-sun-will.

33. "Daniel Webster Quotes." BrainyQuote. Xplore. https://www.brainyquote.com/authors/daniel-webster-quotes.

35. "'He Will Give the Devil His Due' – the Meaning and Origin of This Phrase." Phrasefinder. https://www.phrases.org.uk/meanings/176900.html.

36. Tzu, Sun. The Art of War, Sun Tzu. Place of publication not identified: Simon & Brown, 2010.

38. Voltaire Quotes. BrainyQuote.com, BrainyMedia Inc, 2019. https://www.brainyquote.com/quotes/voltaire_100338

39. Napoleon Bonaparte Quotes. BrainyQuote.com, BrainyMedia Inc, 2019. https://www.brainyquote.com/quotes/napoleon_bonaparte_103585

40. Aristotle Quotes. BrainyQuote.com, BrainyMedia Inc, 2019. https://www.brainyquote.com/quotes/aristotle_140848

41. "Thomas Jefferson Quote: 'If You Want Something You Have Never Had, You Must Be Willing to Do Something You Have Never Done.'" Quotefancy. https://quotefancy.com/quote/168888/Thomas-Jefferson-If-you-want-something-you-have-never-had-you-must-be-willing-to-do.

42. Mark Twain Quotes. BrainyQuote.com, BrainyMedia Inc, 2019. https://www.brainyquote.com/quotes/mark_twain_122378

43. "A Quote by Augustine of Hippo." Goodreads. Goodreads. https://www.goodreads.com/quotes/126110-right-is-right-even-if-no-one-is-doing-it.

44. Henrik Ibsen Quotes. BrainyQuote.com, BrainyMedia Inc, 2019. https://www.brainyquote.com/quotes/henrik_ibsen_149215

45. Thomas A. Edison Quotes. BrainyQuote.com, BrainyMedia Inc, 2019. https://www.brainyquote.com/quotes/thomas_a_edison_109004

46. Friedrich Nietzsche Quotes. BrainyQuote.com, BrainyMedia Inc, 2019. https://www.brainyquote.com/quotes/friedrich_nietzsche_102457

47. "Leo Tolstoy Quote." https://www.azquotes.com/quote/370456.

48. "Jules Renard Quotes." BrainyQuote. Xplore. https://www.brainyquote.com/quotes/jules_renard_147735.

49. "Powerful Motivational Quotes – 8 Keys to Unlocking Your Inner Source of Limitless Potential." The Spiritual Bee RSS. http://www.spiritualbee.com/motivational-quotes/.

50. "Powerful Motivational Quotes – 8 Keys to Unlocking Your Inner Source of Limitless Potential." The Spiritual Bee RSS. http://www.spiritualbee.com/motivational-quotes/.

51. Voltaire Quotes. BrainyQuote.com, BrainyMedia Inc, 2020. https://www.brainyquote.com/quotes/voltaire_132939

52. "Joseph Joubert Quote: 'Our Worries Always Come from Our Weaknesses.'". Quotefancy, quotefancy.com/quote/1057926/Joseph-Joubert-Our-worries-always-come-from-our-weaknesses.

54. Galileo Galilei Quotes. BrainyQuote.com, BrainyMedia Inc, 2020. https://www.brainyquote.com/quotes/galileo_galilei_387486

55. Elbert Hubbard Quotes. BrainyQuote.com, BrainyMedia Inc, 2020. https://www.brainyquote.com/quotes/elbert_hubbard_108523

56. "A Quote by John Mason." Goodreads. Goodreads. https://www.goodreads.com/quotes/21981-you-were-born-an-original-don-t-die-a-copy.

57. Oscar Wilde Quotes. BrainyQuote.com, BrainyMedia Inc, 2020. https://www.brainyquote.com/quotes/oscar_wilde_100486

58. Mark Twain quotations – Criticism. http://www.twainquotes.com/Criticism.html.

59. Moliere Quotes. BrainyQuote.com, BrainyMedia Inc, 2020. https://www.brainyquote.com/quotes/moliere_382611

60. Josh Billings. AZQuotes.com, Wind and Fly LTD, 2020. https://www.azquotes.com/quote/574436

61. Quote by Friedrich Nietzsche: "Those Who Know That They ... www.goodreads.com/quotes/632312-those-who-know-that-they-are-profound-strive-for-clarity

62. Horace Walpole Quotes. BrainyQuote.com, BrainyMedia Inc, 2020. https://www.brainyquote.com/quotes/horace_walpole_163240

63. Soren Kierkegaard Quotes. BrainyQuote.com, BrainyMedia Inc, 2020. https://www.brainyquote.com/quotes/soren_kierkegaard_105030

Made in United States
North Haven, CT
28 December 2023